The Merry Little Christmas
Project & Planner

THE MERRY LITTLE CHRISTMAS

PROJECT & PLANNER

Five Words that Will Transform Your Christmas

Printed in the United States of America

First Printing, 2016
Designed by Sharon Hujik

978-1537679778

www.TheMerryLittleChristmasProject.com

Dedication

For my Mom, who has always made
Christmas merry.

And for the MLCP community – for
inspiring this book in the first place.

Contents

What People are Saying about The Merry Little Christmas Project...

"Thank you for your honest and sometimes funny Christmas experiences. I was feeling alone in my Christmas thoughts when your book crossed my path. It was validating to read that someone else felt like me at Christmastime. I will continue to re-read your book a few months before Christmas and implement your suggestions as the holiday approaches again each year." -Michele

"I just felt it was such a blessing to me this year. I look forward to being a part of the community next year!" -Sharon

"I purchased because this Christmas was not at all what I want it to be. This book has given me hope and a plan for next year!" -Christine

"I just loved the book and really used the ideas to help get ready this year! I know I was able to fit more meaningful activities in this year (like sending cards

– which I love to do) and I will follow the book again next year." -MaryAnn

"This was a very doable way to plan and really made the whole process much less overwhelming." -Christina

"I loved it!!! It's so wonderful to share Christmas prep, ideas, and encouragement with others through-out the season!"-Telena

"Christmas is always a tough time of year for me. I found the Facebook posts to be a bright spot in my day inspiring me to create meaningful gifts and family experiences this year. I must say I had the best Christmas yet. Thank you!" -Nancy

"I thought it was perfect! It freed up my Christmas time. Now I just need a Happy Little Thanksgiving planner to go along with it and all my holiday needs will be met!" -Adelle

Foreword

I have known Kaley for nineteen years. Our friendship began in college somewhere between her famous pumpkin chocolate chip cookies and sharing the deep, dark places in our hearts in our dorm room until the wee hours. And nineteen years later she still brings me her pumpkin chocolate chip cookies across state lines and knows the deepest, dark places of my heart.

One of the things I have always appreciated about Kaley is her desire to be really good at a few things. She doesn't try and keep up with the Joneses, is comfortable in her own skin, knows what she is good at and what she isn't, and will be the first one to admit her weaknesses. And the most beautiful part of this is that she frees me to be me as well – lumps, bumps and all.

And guess what, dear reader? This Christmas, Kaley is freeing you to be you. Not in a Hallmark channel movie kind of way, but in the simplest way you can at the holiday season – freeing you to have the kind of Christmas you will miss in 20 years when your kids are grown.

Part of enjoying Christmas is creating moments. While reading this book, I found myself nodding my head in agreement, saying "Amen" and "Atta girl" all the way though. The over commercialized, "lets-go-into-debt" kind of Christmas always leaves you wanting, unfulfilled and unattached. Kaley outlines simple steps in a non-judgmental way that anyone can take that maybe, just maybe, will change your Christmases forever.

She also offers a planner to help you jump off the tinsel decorated hamster wheel and take practical steps to Christmas sanity and sacredness. So join me in making this Christmas a merry little one.

Beckie Farrant
Author of Infarrantly Creative (infarrantlycreative.net)

THE MERRY LITTLE CHRISTMAS PROJECT MANIFESTO

1. We Choose Less Over Stress

We believe that it's not up to the advertisers and retailers to tell us what our Merry Little Christmas should look like. We get to decide. Often this means that *less really is more.*

2. We Choose the Moments of Christmas

This means that by planning ahead and creating realistic goals, we can *savor the entire Christmas season* rather than just a few hours on December 25th.

3. We Choose Grace

We believe that we will find the kindness, hope and grace we want to pass on to others at Christmastime if we start by *offering ourselves grace first.*

4. We are Better Together

Our online community is our backbone. It provides a place of inspiration and encouragement for those who are on a quest to *Do Christmas Well.*

Join us at TheMerryLittleChristmasProject.com

1

The Year I Cried on Christmas

I remember it well. It was the Christmas of 2011.

We had just finished opening the massive pile of gifts under my in-laws' tree. About 90% of these presents had been gathered, purchased, and wrapped by me — and then schlepped from Pennsylvania to New York on Christmas Eve in our blue Camry.

I remember clearly that we had quite a time trying to cram all the gifts into our little car. We had stuffed and smooshed until each gift was squeezed very carefully into every possible crevice available, and strict instructions were given to limit breathing lest my beautifully wrapped gifts become less perfect in any way.

And now it was Christmas morning, and we were surrounded by the usual piles of torn wrapping paper and bows tossed to and fro, and the strangest thing began to happen to me. I sat surveying the room and all of its chaos. Rather than gratefulness welling up, a small lump in the back of my throat began to form. It was one of those cries that starts in the back of your throat and you try to swallow it down, but then it just keeps growing until it reaches your eyes, and you try to blink it away but instead you find yourself running to hide in the bathroom because really – who is allowed to CRY on Christmas Day?!

Why the Tears?

As I pondered my heavy heart on what was meant to be The Most Joyful Day, I was able to pinpoint three causes:

> 1. The amount of time and energy that it took to pull off Christmas felt monumental (because it was monumental). The positive feedback from my kids? Not so much. Discouragement began to set in as I realized that the reward for all of the emotional energy that I had poured into this day called Christmas was less-than-stellar gratitude.

2. And really – was all this rushing from gift to gift what Christmas was all about? I seemed to remember a far deeper meaning that had very little to do with light sabers or the Xbox or those toys that have a million pieces.

3. I was beyond exhausted. Like so many other years, I had spent the past few nights staying up late to finish last-minute baking, wrapping, packing and all of those other items on a typical Christmas To-Do list for a Mom-Trying-to-Be-Martha-Stewart. It all felt like too much (because it was).

I promised myself in that moment that Christmas would change for our family.

I began to wonder if others might feel as I did about Christmas. I wondered if I wasn't alone in thinking, "this isn't the way it was meant to be."

So, on October 16, 2012, I created a Facebook page titled The Merry Little Christmas Project. At first a few hundred followed, then a thousand, then a few thousand, all joining me in my quest for a simpler, more joyful Christmas.

Together, we've been on a quest to *do Christmas well*. We've shared our triumphs and our failures. We've inspired and encouraged each other. We've learned to love Christmas again.

We've realized we are not alone. Together, we are a joyful force to be reckoned with.

Five Words

Through the years, with the help of this community, I've learned strategies to simplify, organize and make Christmas more meaningful. But more importantly, I've embraced five life-changing words that have transformed Christmas for me and my family:

1. Imperfect

2. Less

3. Anticipation

4. Permission

5. Grace

These five words have helped me love Christmas again. And so, this is the story of how I found my

Merry Little Christmas. Perhaps it will become your story too.

2

Imperfect

Who put the Angry Bird in Jesus' manger?"

It was more of a rhetorical question than anything. The four-year-old and the seven-year-old had some explaining to do.

I laughed, but in full disclosure…I was a little annoyed. I had asked the boys to put their Angry Bird figures away. This was not exactly what I meant, and they knew it.

Let's be honest. I felt a little uncomfortable with how this situation reflected on my parenting skills. I mean, how would Baby Jesus feel? I feared that only irreverent children would place those naughty little birds in such a sacred bed.

On a scale of Kevin McAllister to Tiny Tim, my boys were dangerously close to the *Home Alone* end of the Christmas movie spectrum. They had somehow missed the memo about angelic behavior being required at Christmas time.

A few nights earlier, we had gathered to read by candlelight. Surely the ambiance of the dimly-lit room and the flickering flame would result in a Norman Rockwell–esque moment this holiday season. Instead the two little cherubs spent the majority of the time arguing over which of them would blow out the candle when we were done.

Really?? Didn't they know that this was not how Christmas should be? Did they not realize that Christmas is about peace and joy and well-behaved children? For pete's sake, didn't they know their behavior was not *Instagram-worthy*?!

This Christmas, I was determined that things were going to be different. Not only was I **not** going to cry on Christmas Day, but the entire season would be joyous and delightful and tear-free because that's how Christmas is **supposed** to be. And then, approximately 2.7 seconds into the holiday season, my vision of the Perfect Christmas began to crumble.

There is just something about Christmas that brings out the longing for perfection, isn't there? If you are anything like me, you have visions of reading Christmas stories by the firelight while peace and goodwill abound inside the cozy four walls of your Pottery Barn home. Your family will be a Hallmark commercial come to life, happily reunited, sitting around the table sharing laughter and pumpkin pie. There is very little room in your imagination for such things as stress or family drama or children who fight over candles.

But the truth is, perfection is but a distant dream. And it always will be.

Imperfect

As I envisioned what makes a Merry Little Christmas, I began to embrace the truth that the merriest of Christmases is not marked by the immaculate moments, but everything in between.

As long as I am yearning for a Perfect Christmas, I will always be disappointed. And so, my journey toward a Perfect Christmas began with a step toward imperfection.

I looked at my boys: my Angry Bird pranksters, my candlelight fighters, my _____ (fill in the blank with any number of stresses they will cause me through the years). And I realized something.

This IS how Christmas is supposed to be.

Messy. Imperfect. Full of noise and chaos and sleep-less nights and LEGOs all over the floor and dirt on the rugs and countless moments that don't make it on Instagram. Because that is LIFE, dear reader.

I don't think this longing for perfection will ever go away for me. It likely won't for you either. In this world that highlights and markets the quest for the perfect home, paycheck, and family, we start to believe that perfection is possible if we only try hard enough. **I'm done trying. How about you?**

May I assure you that you'll never experience a Merry Little Christmas until you accept your Imperfect Little Christmas? Where there is life, there is imperfection. So go on: burn the cookies with flair. Wear your ugly Christmas sweater with pride. Laugh at Crazy Uncle Fred's stories that you've been hearing since 1985. Keep lighting that candle and hope that maybe someday those boys will stop fighting over it.

Because that's Life.

Using Your Planner: *On page six, write out a few ways that you will embrace imperfection this year at Christmas. Bonus points if ugly Christmas sweaters make the list.*

3

Less

On the twelfth day of Christmas my true love gave to me twelve drummers drumming,
Eleven pipers piping, ten lords a leaping, nine ladies dancing, eight maids a milking,
Seven swans a swimming, six geese a laying, five golden rings, four calling birds,
Three French hens, two turtle doves and a Partridge in a pear tree.
-Twelve Days of Christmas

I read in an article recently that British women spend 270 hours (11 FULL days) preparing for Christmas.[1] I don't think it's unreasonable to assume that American women log a similar amount of time shopping, wrapping, baking and prepping for this day in December. In another article, I read that you are 5% more likely to suffer a heart attack during the Christmas season than any other time of the year.[2] Call me crazy, but is anyone else thinking there might be a connection between these two stats?

I'm going to step out on a limb here and suggest something wild and wacky:

Is it possible we make Christmas more stressful than it needs to be? Is it possible that in all of our scurrying and hurrying to create a meaningful Christmas, we're actually missing the meaning of Christmas entirely?

Even Dr. Seuss himself admitted that he wrote the book *The Grinch Who Stole Christmas* after recognizing his own dislike of what Christmas had become to him:

> *"I was brushing my teeth on the morning of the 26th of last December when I noticed a very Grinch-ish countenance in the mirror. It was Seuss! So I wrote about my sour friend, the Grinch, to see if I could rediscover something about Christmas that obviously I'd lost."[3] -Dr. Seuss*

Like Dr. Seuss, the next step in my journey toward a Christmas done well was for me to look at myself in the mirror and identify what Christmas had become to me and what it was missing. In doing so, I had to face some difficult realities. The truth was:

- I had become so caught up in acquiring more gifts, more decorations and more stuff that I had very little time to actually revel in the gifts I already have – such as my family.

- I was spending so much money on gifts that I was teaching my kids that Christmas is about getting rather than giving.

- I had become so focused on my perceived needs at Christmas that I had all but forgotten about the needs of those who are lonely and struggling.

- Christmas holds deep meaning for me as a celebration of Christ's birth. There is a beautiful simplicity to his birth story. So why was I making Christmas so complicated??

And here was the biggest eye-opener of all: if I didn't like what Christmas had become to me, it was my own responsibility to fix it. It was no one's fault but my own if I was choosing to make Christmas more stressful and less meaningful than I wanted.

And that's when it hit me.

The advertisers and retailers don't get to decide what my Christmas should look like! A simpler, more meaningful Christmas is actually what my heart really wants! I don't have to listen to those guys! They are not the boss of me!

It was an a-ha moment for sure.

How Much is Enough?

The Christmas our first son was 17 months old, we opted not to get a Christmas tree.

We were first-time parents and in awe of the amount of havoc a small child could create in mere milliseconds. The idea of setting up a tall prickly tree full of glass and lights and things that were fun to break did not seem to be in our best interest. Visions of Christmas Tree Armageddon danced in our heads, and we opted to forego the possible devastation. We also lived in a small above-the-garage apartment, and money was tight. We were trying hard to keep our decorating and gift-giving simple that year.

Then about 5 days before Christmas, I suddenly realized – I really, *really* wanted a Christmas tree. I mentioned it to my husband, and he admitted he was feeling the same way. So we all jumped into our red Jeep Cherokee and drove down the street to a Christmas tree lot – where, thankfully, there were still a few of the tall, prickly things left – and we paid the 10 bucks to make one of them our own.

When we got home, we set it up outside on our deck, safe from the grasp of those precious, ruinous little fingers. We threw some white lights on it and sat in our warm little apartment gazing at its beauty. It was far from fancy, but it was enough. It was LESS and it was enough. We were happy.

This makes me wonder: **who decided that MORE is better at Christmastime?** It's so easy to find ourselves caught up in the, "How much is enough_____to make us happy?" (Stuff, activity, noise, Christmas bonuses, fill in the blank with any number of things).

What if the answer to that is – Less? What if in our quest for *More* what we really want is *Less*?

Like the time I cried on Christmas morning, we suddenly realize that more is just… more. Maybe what we really want is just to be able to soak up and savor that which we already have – but we don't know how.

Less

What if we gave ourselves permission to choose the *less* instead of the *stress* this Christmas?

I had some rather high expectations of myself in regard to Christmas. But the reality was that the size of my Christmas to-do list was so much larger than the joy that it brought. Each item on my checklist represented a little less time that I had left to savor the season. I wanted to figure out a way to get back to *"It was less and it was enough and we were happy."*

And thus, the Christmas To-DON'T list was born.

The Christmas To-DON'T List

You've never heard of such a thing? It's kind of like a to-do list, except it's way cooler since you can cross off each item as soon as you write it down because it's already NOT done! Here is the list that I created to give myself permission to let myself off the hook during the Christmas season. This list is always subject to change, evolve and grow.

1) The Matching-Outfit Christmas Card Photos

I'm not gonna lie. It's a struggle for me to find matching socks for my kids. Matching outfits are but a distant dream, people. I'm going to give myself a pass on this one. I'm pretty sure the rest of the world does not hold me to this standard either. In fact, I'm guessing that if I skipped Christmas cards altogether, my people would understand.

Simple solution: I've discovered that simply creating a collage photo card with candid pics of my family over the year still honors this classic tradition that pre-dates the internets while not offending anyone with my lack-of-family-fashion sense.

2) Exquisitely Wrapped Gifts

Don't get me wrong. I love a creatively wrapped gift as much as the next girl. But my creative-wrapping juices usually dry up after about gift number three. Plus I get all twitchy when my boys take two seconds to tear into the package that I so painstakingly handcrafted. It's like they care more about what's inside or something.

Simple Solution: I lovingly wrap all my gifts in pillowcases or gift bags and save my time for other things. And yes, I'll be the crazy aunt/daughter/sister asking for all of her gift wrap back. Let's just call that being Earth-friendly, shall we?

3) Keeping up with the Joneses

Ahh, Christmas. The most wonderful and guilt-inducing time of the year. From worrying that our kids' feelings will be hurt if their gifts aren't as awesome as the kid's across the street, to comparing our Christmas lights display to the Dad's next door, we sure do know how to pile on the envy during this season of goodwill.

Simple solution: I'm making my new mantra at Christmastime "less is more." While this may not be as simple as I'd like it to be since there are so. many. expectations at Christmas, it sure helps eliminate the envy of anyone else's "stuff." The less time I spend worrying about "stuff", the more time I have to actually enjoy the season.

4) Anything that distracts me from savoring the season

I've learned a lot of things in life the hard way. The first Christmas that I was married, I was determined to get this homemaking thing down, so I attempted to make my own Christmas tree ornaments. It involved a lot more fabric and pins than I was comfortable with.

Thirteen years later and I still haven't finished them.

I have a whole new take on Christmas since then. Simple is good. Whether it be Christmas tree ornaments or cake pops in the shape of Santa for a class party, anything that makes Christmastime more stressful than it needs to be gets stored in the "NOT to do" file.

Simple Solutions: We are going to fill our season with those activities that force us to slow down – reading by candlelight in the evening, driving around to look at Christmas lights, spending time with those who might be lonely. We are still going to bless others and celebrate well, but we'll find simpler ways to do so.

5) Waiting until the last minute to prepare for Christmas

Yes – people like to act shocked and awed when you claim that you have already started Christmas shopping in October. I used to be one of them. But then I was the one crying over my to-do list come December.

Simple Solution: No longer. Giving myself permission to begin my Christmas prep early has changed everything for me. More on this in the next chapter.

I think that before I ever write a to-do list at Christmas time, I will always start with a to-DON'T list.

Why not give it a try? Your list might look different from mine, and that's awesome. But the point is to consider whether your to-do list actually reflects how you want to savor the Christmas season. If it doesn't, it's time to change that.

Less Really is More

Dear reader, I know that you feel weighed down by the Mount Everest of expectations at Christmastime. I know because I felt the same not too long ago. It's exhausting, and far from merry. Something has to give.

Spoiler alert: our time is not nearly as magical as Santa's little red sack and he's actually no help at all at Christmas. So what's going to give? We have two choices. We can acknowledge that we lack both magical powers and elf help; we can plan ahead, eliminate excess activities and simplify gift giving. Or we can try to do all. the. things. and then miss out on the beauty and simplicity of the Christmas season; we can cry on Christmas Day.

Here's the truth. Christmas is going to come no matter whether you get your to-do list done or not. There's freedom in knowing that even when you strip away all of the expectations, the bright lights and the piles of gifts, Christmas still exists. And sometimes letting go of the mountain of expectations is exactly where your Merry Little Christmas starts.

It's where mine started.

Using Your Planner: *Using page eight, create your very own Christmas to-DON'T list. You might want to bookmark it so that you remember NOT to crochet those matching Christmas outfits for your 6 children and 3 dogs this year.*

Notes

1. 1. Euan Stretch, "Christmas most stressful time of year for women as they spend 11 FULL DAYS preparing for it" Mirror.co.uk, December 9, 2013, http://www.mirror.co.uk/lifestyle/family/christmas-most-stressful-time-year-2944946.

2. 2. Michael Lewis, "How to Prepare for a Stress-Free Christmas Holiday Season" Moneycrashers.com, accessed October 15, 2015, http://www.moneycrashers.com/prepare-stress-free-christmas-holiday-season/.

3. 3. https://en.wikipedia.org/wiki/How_the_Grinch_Stole_Christmas!

4

Anticipation

Anticipation. It's my favorite part of Christmas. It's what Christmas – Advent – is all about. Advent is defined as: **"An arrival or coming, especially one which is awaited."** It's meant to be a season of *anticipation.*

When I was young, my mom crafted a countdown-to-Christmas banner out of fabric, string, and twelve Tootsie Rolls. Twelve days before Christmas, she would hang these on the window for each of her six children, and each day we would eagerly unravel the string and pop a fat Tootsie Roll into our mouths.

Tootsie Rolls have never tasted so good. *One more day closer to Christmas. Hurray!*

Somehow, through the years, my tune changed. Instead it sounded something like: *one more day closer to Christmas. Ugh.*

My anticipation for what **was to come** had been replaced by a dread of **what was still to be done**. Visions of sugar plums dancing in my head were replaced by imaginary checklists of what was yet to be decorated, baked, wrapped, purchased, mailed, taped, cleverly and engagingly written, packed or _____ (fill in the blank with any number of verbs).

I don't believe this is the way it was meant to be. How did *anticipation* turn into *dread*? How did the joys of the celebration become a checklist of things-to-be-done? **How did December turn into my least favorite month?** As hard as I tried to do Christmas well, the stress of the season overshadowed the joy I knew I was supposed to feel.

In my search for a Christmas done well, I stumbled upon something that finally allowed me to participate in the wonder of the holiday season just like my children do. And it made all the difference. **Are you ready? My secret to a stress-free December is:**

November.

I used to be the one declaring that the word "Christmas" should not escape our lips until 12:01 a.m. on the day after Thanksgiving and not a second sooner. But now November is my month. I grab my to-do list and knock out as much Christmas prep as possible, all in the hope that I can actually savor the Advent season.

There are three parts to my strategy.

Strategy 1: 20-Minute Missions

20-Minute Missions have changed everything for me. Here's how they work:

Each day in November, I tackle an item on my to-do list for 20 minutes. From Christmas cards to photo projects to decluttering, my goal is that by the end of the month I will have put in hours of Christmas prep without feeling like I did. And the result is that a long to-do list has become a short to-do list.

I've discovered that by setting up a strategy that can be accomplished in bite-sized chunks, I replace the feeling of dread for a looming holiday with a sense of control and competence.

Want to join me? I share my 20 Minute Missions on The Merry Little Christmas Project Facebook page each day in November at facebook.com/The-MerryLittleChristmasProject.

Don't believe me? Here are 20 things you can do in about 20 minutes each to prep for the holidays.

1. Sign up for my *3 Days to an Organized Christmas Challenge* at TheMerryLittleChristmasProject.com. (This one takes 30 seconds, so you have 19 1/2 minutes to do something else!).

2. Bake a batch of cookies for the freezer. (It can be done in 20 minutes. I've done it!).

3. Determine your Christmas budget.

4. Buy a gift online.

5. Buy stamps.

6. Design your Christmas card.

7. Start your Christmas gift list (Amazon Wish List makes this easy).

8. Check your pantry. Make a list of baking supplies you'll need.

9. Decide where you'd like to do your charitable giving this year.

10. Wrap a gift.

11. Put unused toys in a donation bin (or throw away if need be!).

12. Search for simple homemade gifts on Pinterest and pin them.

13. Make a list of supplies needed for any DIY gifts or gift wrap.

14. Organize pictures for photo gifts. Put them all in one file on your computer.

15. Make a list of gift ideas for family, neighbors, or teachers.

16. Make a list of cookies you'd like to make this year.

17. Check your wrapping supplies. Make a list of what you will need.

18. Organize your wrapping supplies.

19. Make a Christmas bucket list.

20. Make your to-DON'T list.

Next comes the second part to my strategy:

Strategy 2: Shopping Complete by December 1st

Sound crazy? Maybe, but it sure beats fighting the masses on Christmas Eve – as I've been known to do a time or two. I've found that crossing this off my to-do list in November is the key to allowing me more time to partake in the wonder of the Christmas season in December.

I'll be honest. This step does require some careful planning. Taking these steps will set you up for success:

1. Sit down and create a list of every present that

needs to be purchased. Be sure to include extended family members, neighbors, teachers – whoever typically receives a gift from you.

Tip: Use pages 16-17 in The Merry Little Christmas Project Planner to help with this step.

2. Simplify. This is the perfect time to assess any ways that you'd like to cut back on gift giving this year. We'll discuss this more thoroughly in chapter 5, but NOW is the time to decide to simplify. As you list out each and every gift that needs to be purchased, you'll likely feel more inspired than ever to do so!

Tip: This step may require contacting extended family to discuss drawing names this year or giving family gifts rather than individual gifts. Sometimes all that is needed is someone to start the conversation.

3. Set up your budget! Based on the amount of money you've set aside for spending, you'll know how much to designate per person.

Tip: Pages 16-17 in the planner can help with this step. I also love to use my Christmas Gift Budget

Spreadsheet to track my spending (http://tinyurl.com/merrylittlenewsletter). It tracks how much I have left to spend per person and helps me stay on budget. If you are a Smartphone user, you may prefer to use a Christmas Planning app for this. Simply search for "Christmas Budget" to find available options.

4. Start gathering lists! My children have no problem with this task, but it's been my experience that husbands struggle with it. (As do wives. Ahem.) You may feel annoying for asking others to plan so early, but better annoying now than stressed-out later!

Tip: Pages 18-25 in the planner offer space to keep track of lists for everyone – family, friends, teachers and more.

Are there usually still a few gifts to buy in those last few weeks? Sure. But this is my biggest stress reliever of them all – and it CAN be done!

Which brings me to my final Mission for the month of November:

Strategy 3: Wrapping it Up

Gone are the days of staying up all hours the week before Christmas to finish wrapping all. those. presents.

I had a brilliant idea a few years ago – why not wrap presents as I buy them instead? Ok, so maybe I wasn't the first person to make this discovery, but whoever did sure was smart.

My goal is to wrap all my gifts during the month of November. I set aside some time each Friday for this task. You might prefer to wrap presents as soon as you get them home or set aside a couple of specific days during the month to accomplish the task. Whatever works for you!

One small word to the wise – be sure to find a way to indicate which gift is which. It's easy to forget by December 25th!

Choosing the Moments

When you take back December, the magic happens. There are endless options for celebrating and savoring the Advent season. Here are some of our favorite ways to do so:

- Lighting a candle each evening while we read our Advent devotional*

- Learning about Christmas traditions around the world*

- Making Bird Seed ornaments*

- Participating in Random Acts of Christmas Kindness*

- Going to a live Nativity

- Baking Christmas cookies (Sign up for my free newsletter to receive my Six Christmas Cookies in 2 Hours Recipes printable plan. You can sign up here: bit.ly/mlcnewsletter.)

- Visiting with friends and family

- Attending our town's Christmas tree lighting

- Having a neighborhood Christmas party

*Check the Additional Resources section in the back of this book for more details.

The way I see it, we can either make Christmas all about one day or we can extend the anticipation into countless joyful moments all month long. I'm learning to choose the moments, rather than the moment. I choose Advent.

Using Your Planner: *There are two parts to this chapter's planning pages:*

- *Use the 20 Minute Missions section on pages 10-13 to map out your daily missions for the month of November.*

- *Create a December Bucket List with your family using pages 14-15. This will inspire you to make the most of November!*

5

Permission

The 1994 version of *Little Women* is one of my all-time favorite movies, and I particularly enjoy watching it at Christmastime. In one of the opening scenes, Meg, Jo, Beth and Amy March praise the Christmas breakfast that their beloved housekeeper Hannah has managed to gather for them in spite of the wartime poverty they are experiencing. "An absolute Christmas miracle!" Meg exclaims. "Isn't butter divinity?" Amy gushes.

Something tugs at my heart every time I watch this scene. I think it may be a twinge of jealousy. I am jealous of their gratitude for such simplicity. I want to be that grateful for butter on Christmas morning.

My, how times have changed. According to an article released by MSN in 2011, American parents now spend an average of $271 per child on Christmas gifts alone.[1] I'm going to take a wild guess that these are the same parents that are complaining about the clutter that has overtaken their home on December 26th.

Why are we so addicted to the belief that Christmas is about stuff?

Honestly, I don't know who the first person was to introduce the idea of a consumeristic Christmas, but I'm confident that the arrival of the Sears Christmas catalog and the evolution of television and internet marketing strategies have perpetuated the ongoing myth that we owe our kids stuff at Christmas.

I can say with certainty that Black Friday's gradual takeover of Thanksgiving Day reflects brilliant marketers strategizing every possible method to get you to spend more money – not less, as they so cleverly like to advertise.

Also. Can we discuss the elephant in the room?

Furby, Tickle-Me Elmo, Cabbage Patch Kids, Teddy Ruxpin, Beanie Babies, Zhu Zhu Pets. THESE are the toys that have caused mass parental panic and nationwide shopping frenzies over the years?

America, come in close. I love you, but this is so disappointing. I need some answers. Why did no one have the presence of mind to say, "HOLD THE PHONE. These things are ugly and I'm afraid they might be staring at me while I'm sleeping"? Why did no one call those sneaky advertisers' bluff and say, "we don't want your creepy toys"? I'm blowing the whistle and calling foul, America.

Christmas marketing is a finely-tuned multi-billion-dollar instrument, with every advertiser fighting to get a bigger piece of the pie. This is why Christmas decorations and gifts are set up next to back-to-school displays at Walmart, and Christmas commercials emerge before the leaves even start changing colors.

Let's face it. Lucy was right. Christmas really is a big commercial racket.

On the other hand, I think giving is beautiful.

In spite of my misgivings about making Christmas all about the presents, I find beauty in giving at Christmastime. I want to see my son's face light up when he recognizes that I know and care about what he likes. I love to view the interactions between my children when they present their gifts to each other. I enjoy letting my friends, neighbors and children's teachers know that they are valued and appreciated.

So the question becomes: how do I honor the tradition of gift-giving at Christmas without becoming another victim of our culture's advertising schemes? How do I turn giving into a meaningful experience and not just an obligation?

Permission

I've realized that the first step is giving myself *permission* to cut back. Here are some hints that there is room for cutting back on gift-giving:

- You are worried that your child will be devastated that his friends got a newer, better, cooler version of the latest hottest technology – and you're referring to your 4-year-old.

- You feel troubled over whether or not your personalized, stenciled and crocheted teacher's-survival-kit-in-a-mason-jar gift is Pinterest-y enough to impress all three of your children's teachers, not to mention the student versions you send for each of your children's classmates.

- The number of people on your list of gift recipients rivals that on Santa's.

- You were one of the parents fist-fighting in Walmart over Beanie Babies.

- You've *ever* felt like you should cut back on gift giving at Christmastime.

The truth is, feeling like you need to change how you give gifts at Christmas might not even have anything to do with how much money you spend.

The first Christmas I felt my giving to be excessive was actually the year that I spent less than $50 total on ALL my gifts. By using my deal-finding ninja skills and setting aside money earned from rewards sites throughout the year, I was still able to snag a LARGE pile of gifts while spending very little of our budgeted money.

But when all the gifts were unwrapped and that inexpensive stash of toys had been scattered throughout the house, I realized I had just put a whole lot of time and energy into buying plain old *stuff*. Since then, I have decided that if I am going to put time and energy into buying gifts, they are going to have to do more than just add another layer of clutter to our home.

Here are some simple strategies that I've discovered to make gift-giving more worthwhile.

Experiential gifts:

Experiential gifts are the best kinds of gifts, in my opinion.

Not only do they reduce the clutter associated with Christmas, but giving the gift of an experience allows the recipient to extend the joy beyond Christmas morning.

There are so many variations on experiential gifts, but here are just a few:

- Aquarium or zoo tickets

- Instrument or sports lessons

- Gift certificate to a favorite restaurant

- Coupon booklet offering various free activities together

- Movie tickets

- Tickets to go bowling, skating, or mini golfing

- A painting or craft class

And the list continues. The options are endless!

The Rule of ONE:

I have a love-hate relationship with Pinterest. I love the endless supply of creative, clever and crafty ideas for gifts. On the other hand, I hate the endless supply of creative, clever and crafty ideas for gifts. It can all get a little overwhelming.

However, Pinterest has changed the landscape when it comes to finding simple (and adorable) gift ideas.

Go ahead – type "simple gift ideas" in the search bar and start pinning!

But what if, instead of feeling like you need to actually use all 1.2 million ideas that you pin, you choose *just one* that will be your go-to gift for neighbors, teachers, and friends? Chances are, they aren't all going to get together to compare notes, so why not?

The Three (or Four!) Gifts of Christmas:

This method of gift-giving has gained some popularity in recent years. Inspired by the idea that Jesus received three gifts when He was born – gold, frankincense, and myrrh – many parents have opted to limit their children's gifts to just three. Others use the four gift rule – which includes "something you want, something you need, something to wear, something to read."

I love how one of my friends makes the most of simplified giving by including a scavenger hunt on Christmas morning as part of the tradition. Giving yourself permission to cut back on the amount of stuff you give doesn't mean you have to cut back on the fun!

As I've given myself permission to simplify gift-giving and focus on more meaningful gifts, I've discovered something. By giving my children less *stuff*, I'm able to give them more of *me*. And quite honestly, I think that's what they actually want in the first place – even if it doesn't make their Christmas lists.

Using Your Planner: *If you haven't yet, take some time to consider your Christmas budget using pages 16-17. Write down every person that you plan to buy for this year and consider ways that you can simplify and make gift-giving more meaningful. Also, no fistfighting this year. Write that down too.*

Notes

1. 1. Amanda C. Haury, "Average Cost of an American Christmas" Investopedia.com, November 22, 2012, http://www.investopedia.com/financial-edge/1112/average-cost-of-an-american-christmas.aspx.

6

Grace

Years ago, my son – then 5 years old – asked for some potato chips after we had finished a meal, even though he hadn't finished his dinner. That night, for whatever reason, I chose to make an exception and allow him to eat the chips.

I decided that I could turn this unusual situation into a teachable moment. So I said, "Griffin, do you know what this is called, when you are given something you didn't really deserve? It's called grace."

Griffin nodded, then proceeded to enjoy every last crumb of the chips. When he was done, he turned his blue eyes up to me and said sweetly, "More grace please!"

Isn't that how we all feel about grace? One serving just isn't enough. Truth be told, I am served up heapings of grace every day. I am surrounded by good things which I did nothing to deserve and so often take for granted:

Loving and supportive family and friends. *More grace please.*

Good health. *More grace please.*

Enough money to put some gifts under the tree. *More grace please.*

Clean running water, a roof over my head and no fear of where the next meal will come. *More grace please.*

The beauty of yet another sunset. *More grace please.*

Dear reader – I gobble up grace each day like it's the whole bag of chips, lick my fingers clean and rarely remember that it is just that. Grace. A gift. By definition, a gift is something that has not been earned, which means grace is risky. Possibly even wasteful.

I was reminded of this truth last Christmas when my family spent an evening surprising others with random acts of Christmas kindness. We had a blast leaving little gifts and treasures to be found around town. I loved watching my kids delight in giving, but I was surprised at something else that I began to feel, something I didn't expect.

It started when my husband and I were discussing who should receive the grocery store gift card that we had just purchased. We scanned the store, carefully analyzing anyone who looked like they could use some Christmas joy, and trying not to make eye contact.

We considered the woman behind the deli counter. She looked like a hard worker. But what if our surprise wasn't as exciting to her as we hoped? What if she just thought we were weird when we walked up to the counter and handed her our gift?

Then, as my sons placed their quarters in the gumball machine, I loved picturing the face of a little one, delighted to find a hidden treasure. But – what if there was a temper tantrum involved and our surprise was just another win for a spoiled child? That's not nearly as much fun to imagine.

There was a chance that whoever found our gift of quarters in the laundry room might seize the opportunity and leave none behind for others. This feeling that stirred in me was not one of kindness. It was more like fear. I worried that our gifts would find themselves in the hands of the wrong person, someone who wouldn't value them like we hoped.

What if those who were meant to be offered a little HOPE this Christmas did not receive our gifts with gratitude?

It is so much easier to be a Recipient than a Giver of *more grace please*, isn't it?

Risky Acts of Christmas Kindness

Giving is indeed risky. And giving without expectation of anything in return is even riskier, whether the recipient is a complete stranger or our own family member. It's true – our gifts might just find themselves in the hands of someone who might not value them as we hoped.

But what's the alternative? Giving because I expect to receive something in return is simply a calculated transaction which just brings continued obligation. That's not the kind of Giver I want to be. I want to give joyfully and not for any benefit that I receive. Christmas offers us that kind of opportunity – if we choose grace.

Grace

What if we allowed ourselves to embrace the humanity of an *imperfect* Christmas?

What if we chose to cut back on the activities and the shopping and the last minute stresses as we celebrate the *less* of the Christmas season?

What if we embraced the beautiful simplicity and *anticipation* of the Christmas season instead?

What if we refused to listen to the marketers and the advertisers, and gave ourselves *permission* to choose a kind of giving that reflects who we are and not who the retailers tell us we should be?

What if we lit candles and sang Christmas songs and loved on those who are hurting and watched the snow fall and paused to breathe in the wonder of our child's delight?

What if?

This kind of Christmas starts with offering yourself grace first. Go ahead. Start there. Then sit back in child-like wonder as you find yourself passing on kindness, hope and more grace, please to others. What if? Just think of the possibilities.

Using Your Planner: *Using page 34, brainstorm ideas for Random Acts of Christmas Kindness you could participate in this year. Let me know if you need my address. Just kidding. Sort of.*

7

Even the Best Laid Plans...

This question came from Pamela on our Merry Little Christmas Project Facebook page a couple weeks before Christmas:

> *"My family had a wonderful, unexpected week-long visit by a family member from out-of-state. Now I'm scrambling to tie up loose ends and it feels over-whelming. Any suggestions on how to complete my decorating, shopping and errands while keeping the spirit of Christmas? I feel like all of my planning was just not good enough and I'm trying not to feel dis-couraged."*

As soon as I read it, I knew I had to share a few things from my heart. You see, as much as I plan and prep and strategize, without fail, a few sneaky unwanted items seem to magically appear on my to-do list at the last minute every single year. As Pamela shared, sometimes life pops up with unexpected (and even welcome) surprises and all the planning in the world can't accommodate the interruptions to our Christmas prep.

So, here is the choice I have to face every year:

Let my last minute Christmas stresses take the joy out of Christmas.

or

Find a way to be okay with the fact that I'm not as prepared for Christmas as I hoped to be.

This is important, dear readers. *All of your planning will only sabotage your joy if your expectations for yourself are too lofty.* Please don't let that happen.

Life is full and messy and imperfect – and so is Christmas. Embrace it. It's likely that not everything will go according to your timeline. Pat yourself on the back for what you have accomplished and move on.

After thinking through my options every Christmas, I realize that I like joy better than stress, so I choose that.

It's not always quite that simple, but here are a few tips that help me overcome the downward spiral of last-minute stress:

1. Write it ALL down.

Get out a piece of paper and a pen and write down everything that still needs to done before December 25th. Then go ahead and cross off anything on your list that is unnecessary. Go ahead. I'll wait.

2. Make it a party.

Have wrapping to do? Pop in a movie, make yourself a cup of cocoa and enjoy the process. Have friends who'd like to join the party? Even better.

3. Take Shortcuts.

Wrap those gifts in dollar-store gift bags, or even better, in pillowcases! Have a 2 Hour Christmas Cookie baking party (get the free printable plan here: bit.ly/mlcnewsletter). Have breakfast for dinner (it's easy!). Find ways to cut corners. You have my permission.

4. Delegate.

You don't have to be Super _____ (Mom, Grandma, Dad, Sister, Aunt, fill in the blank.) If there's something on your list that someone else can do, just ask! (In all honesty, my husband is a better shopper than I am, so asking him to be in charge of some of the shopping is a no-brainer.)

5. PAUSE to enjoy.

When Christmas is all over, it won't be the lack of beautiful wrapping that you regret. It will be NOT taking time to savor the moment. Put away the to-do list and read that Christmas book with your kids, watch that favorite Christmas movie, sing Christmas carols, play in the snow, light a candle for Advent, take a ride to look at Christmas lights. Do it – you won't regret it.

6. Take note for next year.

Don't let this year's stress be in vain. Take note of the things that you want to do differently next year. Let this year make next year better.

7. Most of all, give yourself grace.

Enough said.

And when Christmas Day arrives, remind yourself that a Merry Little Christmas does not come without flaws.

I finally began to grasp this concept on Christmas Day last year. I shared the following on Facebook at the end of the day:

> "Went in to peek at my sleeping boys tonight and got emotional. Our day had its share of chaos and fun. There were children who fought over toys. There were times of laughter and the occasional tears. I was awakened early from my blissful Christmas afternoon nap by one of my boys who shall remain nameless. My middle guy smiled at me multiple times and told me how happy he was it was Christmas. I ate entirely too many Christmas cookies. My little guy snuggled with me and held my hand while watching the Grinch. There were times the house felt too small for all of the bodies, toys, wrapping paper and bows. My mother-in-law bought my oldest son a whoopie cushion. I completely forgot most of the ingredients for the fruit salad I was supposed to make.
>
> It was perfect."

A Merry Little Christmas, indeed.

Using Your Planner: *Pages 36-37 offer you a place to write down your notes for next year. Let this year make next year better! If I had taken notes for next year in 2002, it would say, "Remind yourself next year that you are not comfortable with hand-made ornaments that include too many pins and fabric."*

8

What Christmas Means to Me

The Christmas of 2010 was a good indicator of what was to come on Christmas Day 2011. I remember that I struggled…really struggled…with a sense of being overwhelmed throughout the entire Christmas season. I found myself saying to more than one person, **"It really shouldn't be like this."**

And it's true. It really shouldn't be like this. But it was.

Until one evening about a week before Christmas.

Our advent box activity that evening was to drive around and look at Christmas lights. So we bundled the boys up in warm pj's, grabbed a box of sugar cookies and a camera and loaded everybody into the car.

And we drove. The Christmas music played on the

radio. The boys chirped with excitement. And I mostly just listened. And breathed. (I think I had forgotten to do that for the past few weeks.)

Then we saw it. You know the one. The yard that makes Clark Griswold look like the Grinch. The one that rivals the Disney World Festival of Lights. Or Rockefeller Center. All rolled into one. It was quite the display.

It took me a few minutes, but then I noticed it, way back in a quiet corner behind the Reindeer on the see-saw, and the ginormous Frosty the Snowman, and the Santa riding the Ferris Wheel. It was a nativity scene.

So still. So hidden. So quiet. So different from the noise and chaos surrounding it.

And I was reminded of a truth that I know so well. That the meaning of Christmas is not about the noise and chaos surrounding it. For me, the meaning of Christmas is hidden away, tucked inside a quiet manger.

The meaning of Christmas is HOPE wrapped up in swaddling clothes.

In that moment, I was reminded of the previous Christmas when my oldest son was 4. I'd decided to read the Christmas story to him while he acted it out with our Nativity Scene.

He provided a whole new take on the story. I had no idea that there was so much punching the bad guy involved in the birth of Christ. But to be fair, we read the version that shares how Herod tried to kill Baby Jesus by killing all of the children under two years. He deserved a punch or two.

A few nights earlier, we'd held our own little Christmas pageant at our church. My husband closed the evening by talking about the Upside-Down-Way of Christ.

If I were Jesus, I'm not sure I would have done this story this way. Why God chose to become a Baby and be born in a manger is a bit of a mystery. If I were Jesus, there would be a whole lot more than punching the Bad Guy. The Bad Guy wouldn't have a chance. But it's the way He does things. Upside-Down.

He gives everyone a chance.

He demonstrates real love in the form of this Baby. And He offers Hope. I believe you'll find it in that quiet, hidden manger if you are willing to ignore the noise and the chaos for a minute. *And it's beautiful.*

I wish you a very beautiful and Merry Little Christmas, dear reader.

"And there were shepherds living out in the fields nearby, keeping watch over their flocks at night. An angel of the Lord appeared to them, and the glory of the Lord shone around them, and they were terrified. But the angel said to them, "Do not be afraid. I bring you good news that will cause great joy for all the people. Today in the town of David a Savior has been born to you; he is the Messiah, the Lord. This will be a sign to you: You will find a baby wrapped in cloths and lying in a manger." Luke 2:8-12

Additional Resources

Our Advent Box Activities

One way I have made peace with the ongoing "What are we going to do today, Mom?" question at Christmastime is through our Advent Box tradition.

I bought an Advent Box from Target several years ago containing 25 little cubbies with doors. Each year, I print out some variation of the list below, consult our calendar, and cut the list into little slips of paper to be hidden behind the 25 little doors.

So, when The Question pops up each morning, I smile and direct my children to the door for that day. The day's activity may be as simple as getting out the Christmas mugs, but the tradition helps to reinforce the idea of valuing simplicity. By offering this framework for the month, I also find it helps to eliminate the stress of decision fatigue that can come during such a busy season.

Here is a sample list to offer inspiration if you would like to create your own Advent Box tradition.

1. Hang up stockings

2. Put up Nativity Scene

3. Get out the Christmas books. Choose one to read.

4. Go to a Christmas parade

5. Get out Christmas mugs

6. Make popcorn and hot chocolate

7. Watch a Christmas movie

8. Make a Christmas craft

9. Get out the rest of the decorations

10. Decorate your bedroom

11. Get our Christmas Tree

12. Make Christmas cookies

13. Hang up Countdown to Christmas

14. Shop for gifts to give to Toys for Tots

15. Wrap and deliver Toys for Tots gifts

16. Listen to the story of Christ's birth on CD

17. Begin to read "The Best Christmas Pageant Ever"

18. Put boots out with carrots for St. Nicholas's horses

19. Go to the town Christmas Tree Lighting

20. Make Banana Bread for our neighbors

21. Sleep under the Christmas Tree

22. Go for a drive and look at Christmas lights

23. Read about past Christmases in our book

24. Open our stockings at home

How to Make Bird Seed Ornaments

This gift is for the birds – literally.

Bird seed ornaments also happen to make a fun and thoughtful little gift for the Bird Lover in your life. My kids and I have given these to grandparents and neighbors and they have always been a hit. As a bonus, they take a matter of minutes to put together, with some additional time for the drying.

What you'll need:

- 3/4 cup bird seed (Seed for small birds works great.)
- 1/4 cup water
- 1 small envelope of Knox gelatine
- twine or string
- cookie cutters or mason jar lids
- wax paper

Step 1: Mix together the envelope of gelatine with

¼ cup of water and bring to a simmer while stirring. Continue stirring until the gelatine is dissolved, then remove from heat and cool for a minute. Stir in the bird seed, adding a little more if there is liquid still in the bottom of the pan.

Step 2: Lay the cookie cutter on the wax paper, and fill half way with the bird seed mixture.

Step 3: Cut your twine, knot the end and push the knot down into your bird seed. Then continue filling with bird seed, covering the end of your twine and knot. Push the bird seed evenly into the cookie cutter until it's full.

Step 4: Let them sit overnight to be sure they set. When it comes time to take the ornaments out of the mold, be careful to push them out slowly so you don't lose any pieces!

Makes 2-3 ornaments.

Please note: It is recommended that you let these sit out overnight in a dry room before packaging them, so as to prevent mold. If making them in advance, be sure to store them in an airtight container as well.

50 Random Act of Christmas Kindness Ideas

There is something especially rewarding about surprising people with Random Acts of Kindness at Christmastime. Our Merry Little Christmas community has amazed and blessed me with their own creative RACK ideas they have shared each year via our Facebook page.

Want to join us and need some inspiration? Here are 50 Random Acts of Christmas Kindness ideas for you:

- Make a Card for a Soldier (contact your local Red Cross)

- Write a Thank You Note to someone who might not expect one

- Do Yard Work for a Neighbor

- Pick up litter in your neighborhood – or someone else's

- Make Bird Seed ornaments to give to your neighbors

- Pay for the car behind you at the drive-through

- Leave coins and/or laundry detergent with a note at the Laundromat

- Leave a dollar and a note in the Kids' section of the Dollar Store

- Leave the correct amount of change in a baggie taped to a Redbox

- Write cards to any shut-ins that you know

- Donate needed items to a local food pantry or homeless shelter

- Donate your time to a local food pantry or homeless shelter

- Pay a past due fine for someone at the library

- Donate a special talent of yours to someone in need (crafting, technology, cooking, etc.)

- Smile at everyone you see

- Visit someone in a nursing home

- Adopt a soldier and send a care package

- Donate toys or groceries to a Ronald McDonald House

- Bring a cup of coffee to a friend or someone who is having a rough day

- Leave treats or a gift card for your mail carrier

- Do something special for someone in your family

- Donate to a local animal shelter

- Leave coupons near products in a store

- Tip a server more than you normally would

- Put a quarter in a meter that's about to expire

- Buy stamps for the person behind you at the Post Office

- Donate blood

- Make a date night kit for a couple who needs a break (Redbox code, popcorn, candy, hot chocolate)

- Call someone you haven't in awhile and let them know you are thinking of them

- Have a nice camera? Offer to take family pictures for a family in need

- Make personal care kits for abuse or homeless shelters

- Send a thank you note to your child's teacher

- Donate a gift to Toys for Tots

- Adopt a child from Angel Tree

- Offer to babysit a busy Mom's kids for the afternoon

- Go Christmas caroling in a Nursing Home

- Bring misplaced shopping carts back

- Take a homeless person some food or drink

- Offer to walk someone's dog

- Go spend some time with a shut-in

- Leave a quarter in a gumball machine

- Bring donuts to your local police or fire department

- Organize a neighborhood play date at your house

- Order a pizza to be delivered to a busy Mom

- Write "Have a Great Day" in chalk on your neighbors' driveways

- Find a parking attendant in a cold garage and bring him/her a hot chocolate

- Surprise the cashier when you are shopping and buy him/her a gift card as part of your order

- Set up a Free Hot Chocolate Stand in front of your house for neighbors walking by

- Donate diapers to a crisis pregnancy center

- Buy a gift card for a gas station worker

Christmas Traditions Around the World

Learning about and celebrating various Christmas traditions from around the world is a simple activity that we have enjoyed through the years in our home. Here are some ideas for you if you would like to try the same.

Germany: Children fill their shoes with straw and carrots and leave them outside their front door. It is hoped that when St. Nicholas passes by, he will feed his hungry horses and refill their shoes with apples and nuts. This tradition typically takes place on the evening before St. Nicholas Day which is December 6.

Great Britain: The origin of Boxing Day was in Great Britain. Originally, church alms boxes, filled with donations for the poor, were opened and the money was distributed. They also place crackers (crepe-paper-covered tube with small trinkets inside) by each plate at Christmas dinner.

Australia: Many Australians have made Carols by Candlelight part of their tradition. This involves people gathering, usually outdoors in a park, to sing favorite Christmas songs by candlelight. (We light candles in our fireplace instead!)

Italy: Some families have a tradition of gathering before the manger scene each evening during the nine days before Christmas – the time it is said to have taken Mary and Joseph to make the journey to Bethlehem.

Sweden: A special rice porridge is served at Christmas Eve dinner. Hidden in the porridge is a single almond. Tradition has it that whoever finds the almond in his or her bowl will marry in the coming year.

Mexico: On Epiphany Eve (January 5), children leave their shoes in a window of their homes in hopes that the Magi will fill them with gifts on their journey to Bethlehem.

The Philippines: Traveling minstrels use musical instruments made from coconut shells, split bamboo, and tin-can ends to sing Maligayang Pasko to the tune of "Happy Birthday".

I recommend the book *Christmas around the World* by Mary D. Lankford if you would like to learn more about these and other international traditions.

Our Advent Readings

For years, I struggled to pinpoint the best way to celebrate the Advent season with my boys. We enjoyed
counting down to Christmas with daily activities,
and had created some fun Christmas traditions along
the way.

But the celebration of Jesus' Birth – the Reason why
I celebrate this Season – often became overshadowed by all the activity and chaos, rather than cele-
brated and honored.

Then one Christmas, someone mentioned to me that
they use *The Jesus Storybook Bible* by Sally Lloyd-
Jones as their Advent reading each night. We LOVE
The Jesus Storybook Bible. Its beautiful full color
pages and engaging telling of the story of Jesus
throughout the Bible never gets old. So this sounded
intriguing to me, but I didn't understand how it cor-
responded with Advent.

And then I read a post that pointed out the fact that

there are exactly 24 stories from the beginning of the book to the celebration of Jesus' birth – 21 stories presented from the Old Testament (which "whisper Jesus name") and then the Christmas story is presented in three stories.

24 stories = 24 readings = 24 nights that our family celebrates Advent together before the celebration of Christmas Day.

I'm not sure if this was even intended by the author, but it's brilliant either way.

And then it got even better. Out of the goodness of my sister's heart, she took it upon herself to create clay ornaments for our 'Jesse Tree' that correspond with each of the stories we read each night with the boys. Each night one of the boys pulls out the ornament that is intended for that night's story and hangs it on our "tree" (which for now is a piece of twine hanging on their wall with some clothespins!)

Here is our Advent schedule and the corresponding ornaments:

Dec 1: Creation, Genesis 1-2 (p. 18-27): Earth

Dec. 2: The Fall, Genesis 3 (p. 28-37): Apple with Snake

Dec. 3: The Flood, Genesis 6-9 (p. 28-37): Rainbow

Dec. 4: Tower of Babel, Genesis 11 (p. 48-55): Tower

Dec. 5: The Promise to Abraham, Genesis 12-21 (p. 56-61): Stars in the Sky

Dec. 6: Abraham and Isaac, Genesis 22 (p. 62-69): Ram

Dec. 7: Jacob, Rachel and Leah, Genesis 29-30 (p. 70-75): Sad Woman

Dec. 8: Joseph, Genesis 37-46 (p. 76-83): A Rainbow Coat

Dec. 9: Moses and the Burning Bush, Exodus 3-13 (p. 70-75): A Burning Bush

Dec. 10: Moses and the Red Sea, Exodus 14-15 (p. 92-99): The Split Waters

Dec. 11: The Law, Exodus 16 (p. 100-107): Stone Tablets

Dec. 12: Joshua and Jericho, Joshua 3-6 (p. 108-115): Trumpet

Dec. 13: David's Anointing, I Samuel 16 (p. 116-121): Shepherd's Staff

Dec. 14: David and Goliath, I Samuel 17 (p.

122-129): Slingshot

Dec. 15: David the Shepherd, Psalm 23, 51 (p 130-135): Lyre

Dec. 16: Naaman: II Kings 5 (p. 136-143): A Heart

Dec. 17: Isaiah, Isaiah 9 (p. 144-151): Crown

Dec. 18: Daniel in the Lion's Den, Daniel 6 (p. 152-159): Lion

Dec. 19: Jonah, Jonah 1-4 (p. 160-169): Fish

Dec. 20: The Prophets, Nehemiah 8-10 (p. 170-175): Party Hat

Dec. 21: John the Baptist, Matthew 3 (p. 200-203): A Shell

Dec. 22: Mary and the Angel, Luke 1-2 (p. 176-179): An Angel

Dec. 23: Journey to Bethlehem, Luke 1-2 (p. 180-181): A Scroll (Note: Do not read p. 182 yet.)

Dec. 24: The Shepherds and Wise Men: Luke 2, Matthew 2 (p. 184-188): Star of David

Dec. 25: Jesus is born! Luke 2 (p. 182, 190, 192-198): Three Gifts

*Note that we split the final three readings up to allow us to celebrate Christ's birth on the 25th.

And that is how we celebrate Advent. It's simple and meaningful and I love it.

At the end of a long day, when we pause, light our candle, gently pick out that day's ornament and just listen to the story – it all comes together.

If you would like to learn more about this tradition, along with some pictures and helpful links, you can check out my blog post about it here: http://bit.ly/2bICS7Y

CHRISTMAS
PLANS
20__ __

CHRISTMAS PLANNER

Table of Contents

Additional Resources

NOTES AND IDEAS

Bake in Nov
① for gathering
- dinners
- dessert + coffee

Casseroles/
freezer

Desserts
→ recipes

Soup!

Church

Eve - A playing
Holy Rosary
Maine

Watch Little Women
w/grands

Invite - Ann Marie & Donnas
to CYMC Tea
Linda Lordis

Hot choco/ marshmellows
Fire in fireplace
Candles - safety

Music

Fresh greens
Holly
Agway + free?

INVITE
1. Rita
2. Jack + Lois
3. Pete + Kris
4.

Paint -
annie - candle
Ellia - angel
Syd - rose
or Tiger Eyes

EMBRACING IMPERFECTION

Name a few ways that you will embrace LIFE this Christmas, rather than seeking perfection:

Where there is LIFE, there is imperfection

CHRISTMAS TO-DON'T LIST

QUESTION: Does your to-do list reflect how you want to savor the Christmas season? If not, it's time to change that! List some ways that you are going to let yourself off the hook this Christmas season.

"It's kind of like a to-do list, except it's way cooler since you can cross off each item as soon as you write it down because it's already NOT done!"

- [x] Don't decorate — what?
  Minimize —
- [x]
- [x]
- [x]
- [x]
- [x]
- [x]
- [x]
- [x]

20 MINUTE MISSIONS

What would you like to accomplish now so that you'll have more freedom to savor the Christmas season later?

On the next page, identify the projects that you want to work on, then use pages 12 and 13 to map out your 20 Minute Missions for the month of November.

Example:

Day	Focus
1	This week's focus: Planning
2	Prepare Christmas Planner
3	Write Christmas To DON'T List
4	Begin Christmas lists
5	Prep wrapping supplies
6	Wrap gifts
7	Make a list of ingredients for baking

Use this space for brainstorming:

① Would clothing center like
used Christmas decorations?
PURGE

I'll be sharing my daily missions on The Merry Little
Christmas Project Facebook page so we can help inspire
each other!

20 MINUTE MISSIONS

Day	Focus
1	
2	
3	
4	
5	
6	
7	
8	
9	
10	
11	
12	
13	
14	
15	

"From Christmas cards to photo projects to decluttering, the **goal of 20 Minute Missions** is that by the end of November, you'll have put in hours of Christmas prep **without feeling like you did**."

Day	Focus
16	
17	
18	
19	
20	
21	
22	
23	
24	
25	
26	
27	
28	
29	
30	

BUCKET LIST

What are some ways that you and your family hope to celebrate the Christmas season together this year? Discuss your ideas and create your Bucket List!

"Anticipation. It's my favorite part of Christmas. It's what
Christmas - Advent - is all about."

Budgeting

Take some time to consider and discuss your Christmas Budget this year. Give yourself permission to cut back on spending, if needed. Be sure to include every person and activity that you can anticipate.

Questions to answer:

I have $_____ to spend on Christmas this year.

I will put $_____ towards gifts

I will put $_____ towards travel

I will put $_____ towards meals/special occasions

I will put $_____ towards _____

I will put $_____ towards _____

Think of all the people you want to give a present to this year and list them out. Allocate your budget in the space provided.

Be realistic!

☐ Spouse   ☐ Friends

☐ Children   ☐

☐ Parents   ☐

☐ Siblings   ☐

☐ Teachers   ☐

$50	Mom and Dad		

GIFT IDEAS:

name

gift ideas

FAMILY

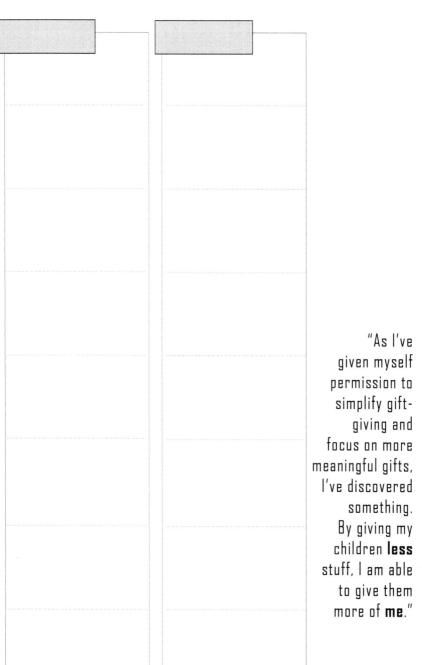

"As I've given myself permission to simplify gift-giving and focus on more meaningful gifts, I've discovered something. By giving my children **less** stuff, I am able to give them more of **me**."

GIFT IDEAS:

name

gift ideas

FAMILY

FRIENDS

name

gift ideas

Teachers, Etc.

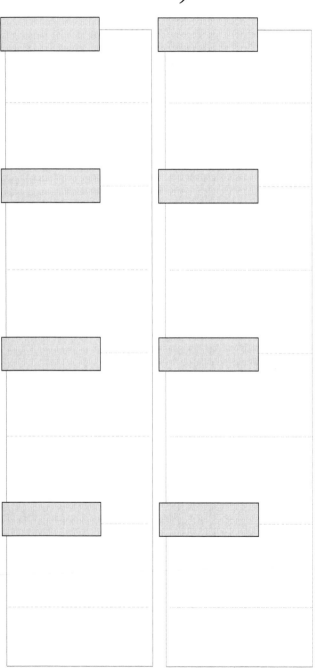

Stocking Stuffer Ideas

name

gift ideas

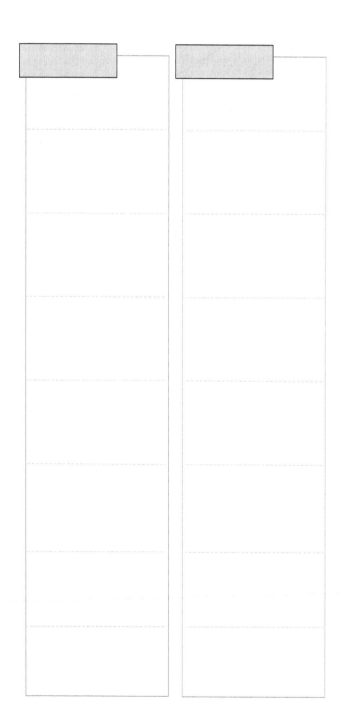

GIFT TRACKER

$ planned	recipient	$25	Kaley
actual spent	gift	$22.99	framed photo
$ remain	purchased? wrapped?	$2.00	purchased? ✓ wrapped?

"So the question becomes: How do I honor the traditions of gift-giving at Christmas? How do I turn giving into a meaningful experience and not just an obligation?"

	purchased? wrapped?		purchased? wrapped?
	purchased? wrapped?		purchased? wrapped?
	purchased? wrapped?		purchased? wrapped?
	purchased? wrapped?		purchased? wrapped?
	purchased? wrapped?		purchased? wrapped?
	purchased? wrapped?		purchased? wrapped?

	purchased? wrapped?		purchased? wrapped?
	purchased? wrapped?		purchased? wrapped?
	purchased? wrapped?		purchased? wrapped?
	purchased? wrapped?		purchased? wrapped?
	purchased? wrapped?		purchased? wrapped?
	purchased? wrapped?		purchased? wrapped?

	purchased? wrapped?
	purchased? wrapped?
	purchased? wrapped?
	purchased? wrapped?
	purchased? wrapped?
	purchased? wrapped?

	purchased? wrapped?
	purchased? wrapped?
	purchased? wrapped?
	purchased? wrapped?
	purchased? wrapped?
	purchased? wrapped?

$ planned	recipient		
actual spent	gift		
$ remain	purchased? wrapped?		purchased? wrapped?

	purchased? wrapped?		purchased? wrapped?

	purchased? wrapped?		purchased? wrapped?

	purchased? wrapped?		purchased? wrapped?

	purchased? wrapped?

$ planned	recipient		
actual spent	gift		
$ remain	purchased? wrapped?		purchased? wrapped?

	purchased? wrapped?		purchased? wrapped?

	purchased? wrapped?		purchased? wrapped?

	purchased? wrapped?		purchased? wrapped?

	purchased? wrapped?

$ planned	recipient		
actual spent	gift		
$ remain	purchased? wrapped?		purchased? wrapped?

	purchased? wrapped?		purchased? wrapped?

	purchased? wrapped?		purchased? wrapped?

	purchased? wrapped?		purchased? wrapped?

	purchased? wrapped?

$ planned	recipient		
actual spent	gift		
$ remain	purchased? wrapped?		purchased? wrapped?

	purchased? wrapped?		purchased? wrapped?

	purchased? wrapped?		purchased? wrapped?

	purchased? wrapped?		purchased? wrapped?

	purchased? wrapped?

RANDOM ACTS OF CHRISTMAS KINDNESS

Write down some ideas that you and your family can participate in this Christmas season:

This kind of Christmas starts with offering yourself grace first. Then sit back in child-like wonder as you find yourself passing on kindness, hope and 'more grace, please' to others. What if? Just think of the possibilities.

NOTES FOR NEXT YEAR

Don't let this year's stress be in vain.
Let this year make next year better.

What worked this year? What didn't? Write it
down and reference this list when you begin to
prep for next Christmas:

Worked Well!	Not So Great

ADDITIONAL RESOURCES

FOOD PLANNING

Cookies and Desserts

Christmas Party

Special Events

Christmas Eve

Christmas Day

Who is Bringing What?

Making a List...

Monthly Goals

January

February

March

April

May

June

"When you **take back December**, the magic happens. There are endless options for **celebrating** and **savoring** the Advent season."

July

August

September

October

November

December

Plans for November

Activities,
Parties and
Traditions:

Monday	Tuesday	Wednesday

Thursday	Friday	Saturday	Sunday

Plans for December

Activities,
Parties and
Traditions:

Monday	Tuesday	Wednesday

Thursday	Friday	Saturday	Sunday

CHRISTMAS PLANS 20__

CHRISTMAS PLANNER

Table of Contents

Additional Resources

NOTES AND IDEAS

EMBRACING IMPERFECTION

Name a few ways that you will embrace LIFE this Christmas, rather than seeking perfection:

Where there is LIFE, there is imperfection

CHRISTMAS
TO-DON'T LIST

QUESTION: Does your to-do list reflect
how you want to savor the Christmas
season? If not, it's time to change that!
List some ways that you are going to
let yourself off the hook this Christmas
season.

"It's kind of like a to-do list, except it's way cooler since you can cross off each item as soon as you write it down because it's already NOT done!"

☑ _____

☑ _____

☑ _____

☑ _____

☑ _____

☑ _____

☑ _____

☑ _____

☑ _____

20 MINUTE MISSIONS

What would you like to accomplish now so that you'll have more freedom to savor the Christmas season later?

On the next page, identify the projects that you want to work on, then use pages 12 and 13 to map out your 20 Minute Missions for the month of November.

Example:

Day	Focus
1	This week's focus: Planning
2	Prepare Christmas Planner
3	Write Christmas To DON'T List
4	Begin Christmas lists
5	Prep wrapping supplies
6	Wrap gifts
7	Make a list of ingredients for baking

Use this space for brainstorming:

I'll be sharing my daily missions on The Merry Little Christmas Project Facebook page so we can help inspire each other!

20 MINUTE MISSIONS

Day	Focus
1	
2	
3	
4	
5	
6	
7	
8	
9	
10	
11	
12	
13	
14	
15	

"From Christmas cards to photo projects to decluttering, the **goal of 20 Minute Missions** is that by the end of November, you'll have put in hours of Christmas prep **without feeling like you did**."

Day	Focus
16	
17	
18	
19	
20	
21	
22	
23	
24	
25	
26	
27	
28	
29	
30	

Bucket List

What are some ways that you and your family hope to celebrate the Christmas season together this year? Discuss your ideas and create your Bucket List!

"Anticipation. It's my favorite part of Christmas. It's what Christmas - Advent - is all about."

BUDGETING

Take some time to consider and discuss your Christmas Budget this year. Give yourself permission to cut back on spending, if needed. Be sure to include every person and activity that you can anticipate.

Questions to answer:

I have $_____ to spend on Christmas this year.

I will put $_____ towards gifts

I will put $_____ towards travel

I will put $_____ towards meals/special occasions

I will put $_____ towards _____

I will put $_____ towards _____

Think of all the people you want to give a present to this year and list them out. Allocate your budget in the space provided.

Be realistic!

☐ Spouse   ☐ Friends

☐ Children   ☐

☐ Parents   ☐

☐ Siblings   ☐

☐ Teachers   ☐

| $50 | Mom and Dad | | |

GIFT IDEAS:

name

gift ideas

FAMILY

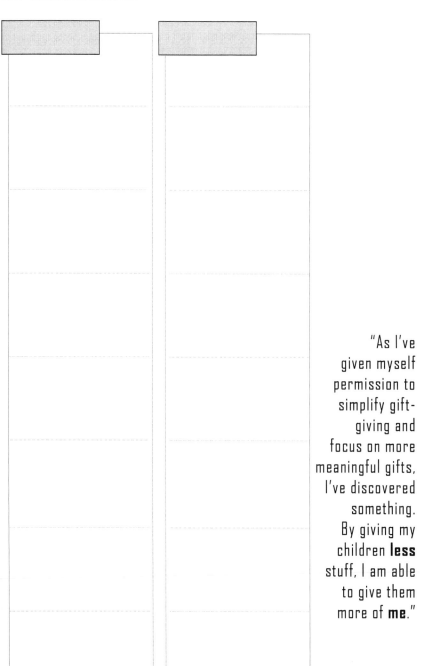

"As I've given myself permission to simplify gift-giving and focus on more meaningful gifts, I've discovered something. By giving my children **less** stuff, I am able to give them more of **me**."

GIFT IDEAS:

name

gift ideas

FAMILY

FRIENDS

name

gift ideas

TEACHERS, ETC.

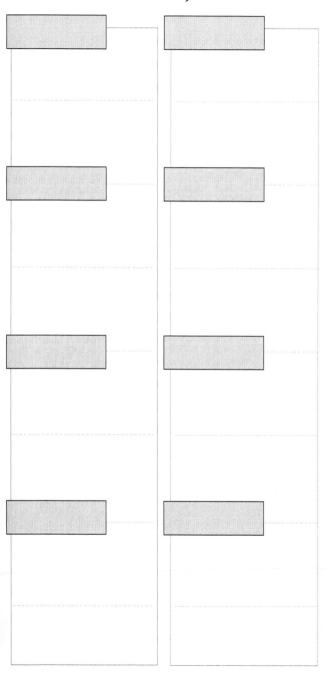

STOCKING STUFFER IDEAS

name

gift ideas

GIFT TRACKER

$ planned	recipient	$25	Kaley
actual spent	gift	$22.99	framed photo
$ remain	purchased? wrapped?	$2.00	purchased? ✓ wrapped?

"So the question becomes: How do I honor the traditions of gift-giving at Christmas? How do I turn giving into a meaningful experience and not just an obligation?"

	purchased? wrapped?		purchased? wrapped?
	purchased? wrapped?		purchased? wrapped?
	purchased? wrapped?		purchased? wrapped?
	purchased? wrapped?		purchased? wrapped?
	purchased? wrapped?		purchased? wrapped?
	purchased? wrapped?		purchased? wrapped?

	purchased? wrapped?		purchased? wrapped?
	purchased? wrapped?		purchased? wrapped?
	purchased? wrapped?		purchased? wrapped?
	purchased? wrapped?		purchased? wrapped?
	purchased? wrapped?		purchased? wrapped?
	purchased? wrapped?		purchased? wrapped?

	purchased? wrapped?		purchased? wrapped?
	purchased? wrapped?		purchased? wrapped?
	purchased? wrapped?		purchased? wrapped?
	purchased? wrapped?		purchased? wrapped?
	purchased? wrapped?		purchased? wrapped?
	purchased? wrapped?		purchased? wrapped?

$ planned	recipient		
actual spent	gift		
$ remain	purchased? wrapped?		purchased? wrapped?

	purchased? wrapped?		purchased? wrapped?

	purchased? wrapped?		purchased? wrapped?

	purchased? wrapped?		purchased? wrapped?

	purchased? wrapped?

$ planned	recipient		
actual spent	gift		
$ remain	purchased? wrapped?		purchased? wrapped?

	purchased? wrapped?		purchased? wrapped?

	purchased? wrapped?		purchased? wrapped?

	purchased? wrapped?		purchased? wrapped?

	purchased? wrapped?

$ planned	recipient		
actual spent	gift		
$ remain	purchased? wrapped?		purchased? wrapped?

	purchased? wrapped?		purchased? wrapped?

	purchased? wrapped?		purchased? wrapped?

	purchased? wrapped?		purchased? wrapped?

	purchased? wrapped?

$ planned	recipient		
actual spent	gift		
$ remain	purchased? wrapped?		purchased? wrapped?

	purchased? wrapped?		purchased? wrapped?

	purchased? wrapped?		purchased? wrapped?

	purchased? wrapped?		purchased? wrapped?

	purchased? wrapped?

RANDOM ACTS OF CHRISTMAS KINDNESS

Write down some ideas that you and your family can participate in this Christmas season:

This kind of Christmas starts with offering yourself grace first. Then sit back in child-like wonder as you find yourself passing on kindness, hope and 'more grace, please' to others. What if? Just think of the possibilities.

NOTES FOR NEXT YEAR

Don't let this year's stress be in vain.
Let this year make next year better.

What worked this year? What didn't? Write it
down and reference this list when you begin to
prep for next Christmas:

Worked Well!	Not So Great

ADDITIONAL RESOURCES

Food Planning

Cookies and Desserts

Christmas Party

Special Events

Christmas Eve

Christmas Day

Who is Bringing What?

Making a List...

MONTHLY GOALS

January

February

March

April

May

June

"When you **take back December**, the magic happens. There are endless options for **celebrating** and **savoring** the Advent season."

July

August

September

October

November

December

Plans for November

Activities,
Parties and
Traditions:

Monday	Tuesday	Wednesday

Thursday	Friday	Saturday	Sunday

Plans for December

Activities,
Parties and
Traditions:

Monday	Tuesday	Wednesday

Thursday	Friday	Saturday	Sunday

CHRISTMAS
PLANS
20__

CHRISTMAS PLANNER

Table of Contents

Additional Resources

NOTES AND IDEAS

EMBRACING IMPERFECTION

Name a few ways that you will embrace LIFE this Christmas, rather than seeking perfection:

Where there is LIFE, there is imperfection

CHRISTMAS
TO-DON'T LIST

QUESTION: Does your to-do list reflect
how you want to savor the Christmas
season? If not, it's time to change that!
List some ways that you are going to
let yourself off the hook this Christmas
season.

"It's kind of like a to-do list, except it's way cooler since you can cross off each item as soon as you write it down because it's already NOT done!"

✓ _____

✓ _____

✓ _____

✓ _____

✓ _____

✓ _____

✓ _____

✓ _____

✓ _____

20 MINUTE MISSIONS

What would you like to accomplish now so that you'll have more freedom to savor the Christmas season later?

On the next page, identify the projects that you want to work on, then use pages 12 and 13 to map out your 20 Minute Missions for the month of November.

Example:

Day	Focus
1	This week's focus: Planning
2	Prepare Christmas Planner
3	Write Christmas To DON'T List
4	Begin Christmas lists
5	Prep wrapping supplies
6	Wrap gifts
7	Make a list of ingredients for baking

Use this space for brainstorming:

I'll be sharing my daily missions on The Merry Little Christmas Project Facebook page so we can help inspire each other!

20 MINUTE MISSIONS

Day	Focus
1	
2	
3	
4	
5	
6	
7	
8	
9	
10	
11	
12	
13	
14	
15	

"From Christmas cards to photo projects to decluttering, the **goal of 20 Minute Missions** is that by the end of November, you'll have put in hours of Christmas prep **without feeling like you did**."

Day	Focus
16	
17	
18	
19	
20	
21	
22	
23	
24	
25	
26	
27	
28	
29	
30	

Bucket List

What are some ways that you and your family hope to celebrate the Christmas season together this year? Discuss your ideas and create your Bucket List!

"Anticipation. It's my favorite part of Christmas. It's what Christmas - Advent - is all about."

BUDGETING

Take some time to consider and discuss your Christmas Budget this year. Give yourself permission to cut back on spending, if needed. Be sure to include every person and activity that you can anticipate.

Questions to answer:

I have $_____ to spend on Christmas this year.

I will put $_____ towards gifts

I will put $_____ towards travel

I will put $_____ towards meals/special occasions

I will put $_____ towards _____

I will put $_____ towards _____

Think of all the people you want to give a present to this year and list them out. Allocate your budget in the space provided.

Be realistic!

☐ Spouse   ☐ Friends

☐ Children ☐

☐ Parents   ☐

☐ Siblings ☐

☐ Teachers ☐

$50	Mom and Dad		

GIFT IDEAS:

name

gift ideas

FAMILY

"As I've given myself permission to simplify gift-giving and focus on more meaningful gifts, I've discovered something. By giving my children **less** stuff, I am able to give them more of **me**."

GIFT IDEAS:

name

gift ideas

FAMILY

FRIENDS

name

gift ideas

Teachers, Etc.

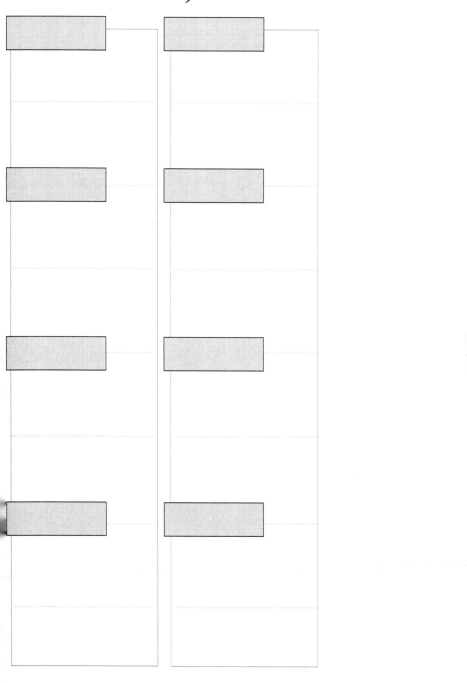

STOCKING STUFFER IDEAS

name

gift ideas

GIFT TRACKER

$ planned	recipient	$25	Kaley
actual spent	gift	$22.99	framed photo
$ remain	purchased? wrapped?	$2.00	purchased? wrapped?

"So the question becomes: How do I honor the traditions of gift-giving at Christmas? How do I turn giving into a meaningful experience and not just an obligation?"

	purchased? wrapped?		purchased? wrapped?
	purchased? wrapped?		purchased? wrapped?
	purchased? wrapped?		purchased? wrapped?
	purchased? wrapped?		purchased? wrapped?
	purchased? wrapped?		purchased? wrapped?
	purchased? wrapped?		purchased? wrapped?

	purchased? wrapped?		purchased? wrapped?
	purchased? wrapped?		purchased? wrapped?
	purchased? wrapped?		purchased? wrapped?
	purchased? wrapped?		purchased? wrapped?
	purchased? wrapped?		purchased? wrapped?
	purchased? wrapped?		purchased? wrapped?

	purchased? wrapped?		purchased? wrapped?
	purchased? wrapped?		purchased? wrapped?
	purchased? wrapped?		purchased? wrapped?
	purchased? wrapped?		purchased? wrapped?
	purchased? wrapped?		purchased? wrapped?
	purchased? wrapped?		purchased? wrapped?

$ planned	recipient		
actual spent	gift		
$ remain	purchased? wrapped?		purchased? wrapped?

	purchased? wrapped?		purchased? wrapped?

	purchased? wrapped?		purchased? wrapped?

	purchased? wrapped?		purchased? wrapped?

	purchased? wrapped?

$ planned	recipient		
actual spent	gift		
$ remain	purchased? wrapped?		purchased? wrapped?

	purchased? wrapped?		purchased? wrapped?

	purchased? wrapped?		purchased? wrapped?

	purchased? wrapped?		purchased? wrapped?

	purchased? wrapped?

$ planned	recipient		
actual spent	gift		
$ remain	purchased? wrapped?		purchased? wrapped?

	purchased? wrapped?		purchased? wrapped?

	purchased? wrapped?		purchased? wrapped?

	purchased? wrapped?		purchased? wrapped?

	purchased? wrapped?

$ planned	recipient		
actual spent	gift		
$ remain	purchased? wrapped?		purchased? wrapped?

	purchased? wrapped?		purchased? wrapped?

	purchased? wrapped?		purchased? wrapped?

	purchased? wrapped?		purchased? wrapped?

	purchased? wrapped?

Random Acts of Christmas Kindness

Write down some ideas that you and your family can participate in this Christmas season:

This kind of Christmas starts with offering yourself grace first. Then sit back in child-like wonder as you find yourself passing on kindness, hope and 'more grace, please' to others. What if? Just think of the possibilities.

NOTES FOR NEXT YEAR

Don't let this year's stress be in vain.
Let this year make next year better.

What worked this year? What didn't? Write it
down and reference this list when you begin to
prep for next Christmas:

Worked Well!	Not So Great

ADDITIONAL RESOURCES

Food Planning

Cookies and Desserts

Christmas Party

Special Events

Christmas Eve

Christmas Day

Who is Bringing What?

Making a List...

MONTHLY GOALS

January

February

March

April

May

June

"When you **take back December**, the magic happens. There are endless options for **celebrating** and **savoring** the Advent season."

July

August

September

October

November

December

Plans for November

Activities,
Parties and
Traditions:

Monday	Tuesday	Wednesday

Thursday	Friday	Saturday	Sunday

Plans for December

Activities,
Parties and
Traditions:

Monday	Tuesday	Wednesday

Thursday	Friday	Saturday	Sunday

Made in the USA
Middletown, DE
10 October 2016